Amazing But True Fishing Stories

D0514524

Amazing but True Fishing STORIES

Bruce Nash and Allan Zullo

Compiled by Ray Villwock

Andrews and McMeel · *A Universal Press Syndicate Company* · Kansas City

Designed by Rick Cusick.
Illustrations by Paul Coker, Jr.

Library of Congress Cataloging-in-Publication Data

Nash, Bruce M.
      Amazing but true fishing stories / Bruce Nash and Allan Zullo ;
      compiled by Ray Villwock.
        p. cm.
      ISBN 0-8362-8022-9 : $6.95
      1. Fishing. 2. Fishing—Records. I. Zullo, Allan.
    II. Villwock, Ray. III. Title.
    SH441.N37   1993
    799.1—dc20   92-34622
                                                         CIP

First Printing, February 1993
Second Printing, July 1993

Attention: Schools and Businesses
Andrews and McMeel books are available at quantity discounts with bulk purchase for educational, business, or sales promotional use. For information, please write to: Special Sales Department, Andrews and McMeel, 4900 Main Street, Kansas City, Missouri 64112.

Dedication

To my friend Phil Gurin: Keep casting your
creative ideas in the unpredictable waters of
television and some day you will land the big one.
—*Bruce Nash*

To my son-in-law Danny Manausa with hopes that
you hook your goals and land your dreams.
—*Allan Zullo*

To Judi, who is both amazing and true.
—*Ray Villwock*

Acknowledgments

We wish to thank the many professional and amateur anglers, guides, boat captains, and outdoor writers who contributed to this book. We are especially grateful to: Brandon Bolinski, Ted Dzialo of the National Fresh Water Fishing Hall of Fame, Sugar Ferris of Bass'n Gals, Janice Gregory, Mike Leech of the International Game Fish Association, Ann Lewis of B.A.S.S., Joe Mullins, Steve Plamann, Dr. James R. Pritchard, Mick Thill, and Mireya Throop.

Contents

Perhaps in no other sport is the line separating fact and fiction so fuzzy. *Anglers are as likely to tell a fish tale as they are to tag a fish tail.*

However, as you are about to find out, in fishing, truth is often more amazing than fiction. This book is a celebration of real people and events in the world of fishing that we hope will astound, baffle, and amuse you. Like the angler who used his rod and reel to hook and save a drowning woman . . . the young boy who went fishing for 1,262 straight days . . . the trout that was kept in jail for two years . . . the anglers who caught eighty-three sailfish in one day . . . the school of fish that rained down from the sky.

What makes an incident so incredible, a feat so fantastic, or a record so remarkable is often nothing more than good luck . . . or bad luck. For example, a Frenchman using one pole once pulled in 590 fish in an hour, but an American battled a monster salmon for thirty-seven hours and then lost it. One lucky tournament angler landed a single fish worth $65,000, but an unfortunate fisherman lost over $20,000 in tourney prizes simply because he wore the wrong hat.

And that's what makes fishing so appealing. It's the sport where the most amazing things can—and do—happen.

Reel Battles
Thrilling Duels with Fighting Fish

Battle Royale

Bob Ploeger hooked a world-record salmon. But before the battle for the prize was over, he had fought the fish from three different boats, become a star of local radio and television, and smashed the record for the longest fight ever with a fish.

Ploeger dueled with the fish—estimated at over 100 pounds—for a grueling thirty-seven hours! But then, just as his finny foe was about to be netted, an angler's worst fear was realized—the fish broke free.

For Ploeger, a sixty-three-year-old retired prison guard from Minnesota, it was a bittersweet ending to his lifelong dream of fishing in Alaska.

"My wife and I promised ourselves that when I retired, we'd go and do some fishing for the 'Big One,'" said Ploeger. "But we never dreamed how big it would be."

On July 12, 1989, Ploeger was on a half-day fishing trip with guide Dan Bishop in a rowboat on the Kenai River near Anchorage. Because Ploeger hadn't caught anything all morning, Bishop let him continue to fish past noon.

1

At 12:30 P.M., Ploeger got a strike . . . and the greatest fight between man and fish began.

"I knew it was a big fish right away," Ploeger recalled. The fish stayed motionless on the bottom of the river for ninety minutes before it started to move away. Bishop began rowing frantically to keep up with the fish. But then it changed direction and began going upstream into fast water.

Bishop couldn't row the boat against the strong current and it looked like the fight would end early until a friendly fisherman in a sixteen-foot motorboat nearby saw what was happening and switched boats with Bishop and Ploeger.

The two were then able to follow the fish up the rapids before it doubled back and headed five miles downstream. At 5 P.M., the fish surfaced for the first time, and Bishop saw that it was a record-breaking king salmon.

Friends brought gas out to the boat so Bishop could continue holding the vessel steady in the current. The local radio station began broadcasting live reports from the river every fifteen minutes while an Anchorage television station sent a camera crew to cover the struggle.

By now, the banks were lined with spectators. The local McDonald's and Coca-Cola dealer sent refreshments to the two anglers, who then switched to a larger, more comfortable third boat, a twenty-footer.

Meanwhile, the salmon played possum, barely moving for hours at a time. Darkness came and went, and with the morning light the guide decided on a different strategy. Using a

spare oar, he began jabbing at the bottom of the river, hoping to stir the fish into action. But throughout the second day, the salmon moved only 150 yards. "There was a whole fleet of boats around us and TV cameras and spectators were all along the banks," recalled Ploeger. "They started cheering around 8:30 P.M., when a radio reporter announced we'd now beaten the record of thirty-two hours for the longest time spent playing a fish. I was kind of embarrassed that all these people were watching me.

"I never slept the entire time. And I really didn't feel that sleepy. I never gave up the rod. This was a fish of a lifetime and I'm retired, so I knew I'd have plenty of time to rest after I reeled him in. It never even occurred to me to take a nap."

Soon after midnight, Friday, July 14, the great fish began to move again. The anglers asked the television crew to shine their lights on the fish. There, two feet below the surface, they got another good look at a salmon that might be worth a million dollars in endorsements and guide business.

They could also see that the line was badly frayed and wouldn't last much longer.

"We were desperate," said Bishop. "We knew there was a good chance the fish could snag the line or break it. We decided our best plan was to try to net him before he got away."

Carefully, Bishop tried to slip a four-foot net around the salmon's tail, at the same time that a second guide who had boarded the boat tried to net the fish from its head. A third guide handled the controls on the boat.

Suddenly, the salmon jerked its head and the orange lure fell out. "For the longest moment I've ever known, he was there in the river, not held by the nets, but not free of them either," said Bishop.

The weight of the salmon bent both net frames so that neither guide could lift the fish into the boat. With a gentle swish of its tail, the salmon rolled out of the nets and slipped away.

After thirty-seven exhausting hours, Ploeger had nothing to show for his marathon battle except aching muscles and an empty line. The angler, who had never caught anything larger than a twelve-pounder, took the loss hard at first.

"But then I reasoned I always pray to God to let me just have a good time when I go fishing. I don't pray that he'll send me a big fish. So I thanked the Lord that he'd given me such a memorable experience that I will never forget—and a great tale to tell my nine grandchildren."

A Fisherman's Last Stand

Dennis Dunn fought a giant blue marlin for thirty hours—while standing up the whole time!

Dunn, an American, was fishing in the New Zealand Open Championship when the unique battle began. He was aboard a boat rigged for bottom-fishing, so it didn't have a fighting chair. But at 9:30 A.M. on February 18, 1988, he hooked a monster marlin estimated at 1,200 pounds on his fifty-pound test bottom outfit.

The marlin was so strong that it towed the boat more than forty miles during the long ordeal that followed. Meanwhile, Dunn stood up for thirty straight agonizing hours and never once let go of his rod. He was fed oranges and other food to keep up his strength, and a doctor was brought aboard to treat him for blistered hands, sunburn, and fatigue.

But after thirty hours and five minutes, the exhausted Dunn conceded defeat and surrendered the rod to other fishermen aboard the boat. They battled the marlin for two more hours, but the fish was still going strong. Finally, and reluctantly, the boat's captain ended the fight when he ordered the line cut. The marlin had won.

Three on a Catch

In one of the strangest fishing battles ever, a bluefish and a sea gull dueled over a mullet—and both lost.

One day in 1979, Stephen Baffic, of Arlington, Texas, was surf-fishing at Cape May, New Jersey, when a school of bluefish suddenly began crashing bait in the surf. He cast his rig, baited with a mullet on each of two hooks, toward the action. While the bait was still flying through the air, a sea gull grabbed one of the mullet and became entangled in Baffic's line.

At about the same time, a seven-pound bluefish hit the other mullet, and the battle was on. The sea gull pulled one way and the big blue the other. Baffic fought both of them, but made little headway.

At first, no one gained much ground in the three-way struggle. But after twenty minutes, Baffic prevailed, beaching both the sea gull and the bluefish.

The bird was released unharmed. The fish went to the frying pan. And Baffic had an amazing—but true—fishing story to tell!

Spearing a Record

Don Pinder came face-to-face with a fish underwater that was four times bigger than he was—yet he managed to kill it by hand.

Pinder, of the Miami Triton Club, was spearfishing in the Atlantic Ocean in 1955 when he encountered an 804-pound jewfish. He successfully speared it and put his name in the record books.

Paying the Lone Shark

A hooked tiger shark put up such a fierce battle that it defeated the valiant efforts of three fishermen and a captain and damaged their boat before breaking free.

   In 1978, off Destin, Florida, Captain Buddy LaPointe and three anglers entered a shark-fishing tournament. At 3 A.M., a fourteen-foot, 1,000-pound-plus tiger shark hit their bait, a ten-pound bonito. The fishermen took turns fighting the shark, using fifteen feet of braided cable leader on the end of their line.

   "I knew it was going to be a long night when the shark tore the first fighting chair right out of the floor," Captain LaPointe recalled. For the next three and a half hours, the shark proceeded to destroy two gimbals (rod holders) off two other fighting chairs, break the strap on a shoulder harness, and wreck a fighting belt worn by one of the fishermen.

One by one, the shark wore out each of the three anglers before Captain LaPointe took over the line. But he couldn't do any better.

At 6:30 A.M., the fighting fish broke the line and swam free.

At 6:31 A.M., three whipped fishermen, a tired captain, and an extremely battered boat headed for safe harbor—without their prize catch.

The Life You Save . . .

Brian Bird had to choose between the giant flathead catfish he was fighting and saving his own life. He chose to live.

While fishing below the dam on Oklahoma's Lake Overholser in 1987, Bird hooked the flathead, estimated at about forty pounds, and fought it for nearly ten minutes. Suddenly, the fish jerked hard and tugged Bird into the fast-moving current.

The angler now had a new battle to wage—for his life. Bird was swept away in a violent undertow just below the dam. He quickly surrendered his rod and reel to the fish and tried desperately to stay afloat.

Through the spray of the churning water, Bird spotted a sandbar fifty yards away. With all the strength he could muster, he swam toward safety. But twice he was pulled under by the raging current. Finally, Bird struggled to the small sandbar and collapsed from exhaustion.

He remained stranded for two hours before he was rescued by an emergency team.

Now That's Sailsmanship!

John Cacciutti dove into the water to snare his prize catch—after it had swiped his rod and reel!

During a vacation in Acapulco, Mexico, in 1989, Cacciutti, of Wallingford, Pennsylvania, his wife Terry, and four friends chartered a boat and went looking for sailfish. Within a couple of hours, Terry and a friend had each caught two sails. Everyone was having a good time as Cacciutti settled into a chair on the bridge of the boat, sipping a cool drink.

Suddenly, like the crack of a whip, the rod in the bridge rod-holder snapped from the outrigger and started dumping line at an alarming rate. Cacciutti quickly pointed the rod at the fish, locked up the drag, and set the hook hard. "Up out of the water came a beautiful nine-foot Pacific sailfish," he recalled. "The bridge was a great vantage point to watch this aerial action, but it was no place to fight a fish. I needed to get back down on deck."

Cacciutti took the rod and reel and started down the ladder when he slipped and fell onto the deck below.

"Unfortunately, the rod and reel didn't make this journey with me," he recalled. "As I was falling, I tried to pull a six-foot rod sideways through a three-foot ladder hole, but the rod had its own idea and shot from the bridge like an arrow. We all watched in amazement as the rod sailed high over our heads and splashed into the water."

Then they saw the sailfish make a few jumps before sounding into 1,000 feet of water. While Cacciutti sulked and tried to shake off his embarrassment, one of his friends on the bow spotted the sailfish still dragging the rod and reel. The boat pursued the fish and came close to it several times, but each time the sailfish sounded again.

"All the hopes and dreams I had of recapturing that fish quickly faded," Cacciutti said. "I went to the bow and stared into the deep blue water as thoughts of defeat raced through my mind. Suddenly, I spotted the fish again next to the boat. I knew there was no more time for thought or words to the crew.

"I dove off the starboard bow with my hands outstretched and hit the water behind the big fish. I swam about twenty feet down and grabbed onto the taut fishing line. With my lungs about to burst, I made it to the surface for a breath of air.

"Meanwhile, the big fish was running away from me and the line was burning my hand. But then the line slowly became slack and I began to worry about the fish and its sixteen-inch bill. Could it be charging me this very second? My heart was pumping from fear as I swam toward the boat. But fortunately the sail didn't charge and I climbed back onto the deck."

Once on board, Cacciutti continued to pull in the line hand over hand until, up from the depths, sprang the rod and reel. The soaking-wet angler grabbed hold of the rod with two hands, quickly took in the slack, and pulled and cranked in 1,000 feet of line. Finally, he reeled in the tired fish until it was alongside the boat. With heavy gloves on his hands, the first mate then leaned over the side and grabbed hold of the bill of the sailfish.

"I got a baseball bat and was ready to subdue the fish," said Cacciutti, "when the captain and his mate shouted for me to release it. After thinking about it, I decided that the greatest trophy would be in the pictures that my wife was taking and the story about this catch. There was no need to kill this great fish."

After measuring the sail, they pulled it along in the water, forcing water through its gills, which helped to revive it. "The fish began to move his big tail, so we gave him a push and set him free," said Cacciutti. "The sailfish returned to the sea to fight again."

Holy Mackerel!
Fantastic Fishing Feats

Twin Fins

Identical twins Gina and Toni Grimaldi are so much alike they have even caught identical fish!

In 1984, when the girls from Springfield, Massachusetts, were fifteen years old, they went on a charter boat to fish off the coast of Bermuda.

Using 130-pound tackle, Toni hooked a blue marlin and fought it for thirty-eight minutes before bringing a 187-pound keeper to gaff.

Two hours later, Gina got a hit on her 80-pound tackle. Just like her twin, Gina snared a blue marlin. And just like her twin, Gina battled it for thirty-eight minutes. And unbelievably, just like her twin, Gina landed a keeper that weighed 187 pounds!

Sail of the Century

In one of the greatest feats in sport fishing, anglers aboard the charter boat *Elbo Seven* caught and released an eye-popping eighty-three sailfish—in one day!

On February 3, 1980, Captain Al Johnston was taking fishermen Ozzie Boski and Bo Trossbach a few miles off the shore of Boynton Beach, Florida, when they came across hundreds of sailfish in groups of six to twenty circling tightly herded balls of sardines.

The anglers decided to see how many fish they could catch and release. The fishing began in earnest at 10 A.M. after first mate Pete Wright grabbed a seven-foot dip net and scooped deep into the pod of sardines and came up with enough bait for the whole day.

Within one and a half hours, Boski and Trossbach had caught twenty-one sails on live sardines. The first blitz ended, however, when bonito moved in and the sailfish sounded. So the anglers headed north until they found more balls of baitfish off Palm Beach. "Schools of bait were everywhere and so were the sails—literally churning the water," said Johnston.

The fishermen were pulling in sail after sail. As the rally wore on, Wright was rigging double line to sixty- and eighty-pound monofilament leaders. For the next four hours, he threaded hooks through bait and tied dozens of Bimini knots. Whenever an angler caught a sail, Wright grabbed the line, cut it, and got ready for the next sailfish.

Almost every fish, weighing from forty-five to sixty pounds each, was hooked and released within five minutes. The numbers of sails caught kept climbing . . . fifty . . . sixty . . .

seventy. . . . Finally, with backs aching, fingers bleeding, and muscles straining, the fishermen called it quits.

Their incredible score: eighty-three sailfish.

"You couldn't believe it unless you were there," said Wright. Because there weren't enough red release flags on board, Wright penned the number "83" on a white flag and flew it from the center rigger as they headed home. Said Wright, "It was the Super Bowl of fishing, the rally of all time."

True Grit

Pro Bass'n Gal angler Cindy Caperton was determined to get to the weigh-in with her catch—even though it meant being dragged through freezing water while holding onto the side of her boat.

But it was worth it. Cindy's gritty toughness helped her to a Top 10 finish in the 1988 Bass'n Gal tournament at Lake Fork in Texas.

Cindy had a feeling it was going to be a tough day when her boat's engine wouldn't turn over that morning. She and her fishing partner needed a jump start and, as a result, they headed out last—to a remote little creek that nobody else bothered to fish. Two hours later, their trolling motor malfunctioned and they were reduced to pulling the boat along the edge of the bank by grabbing overhanging branches.

Still, Cindy managed to land two good bass and—considering it was a cold, windy day—she was pleased. They had an hour to get back to the weigh-in, which seemed like plenty of time.

However, once again, the engine wouldn't start. But that didn't stop Cindy. "All I could think to do was jump in and swim the boat out of the creek to the main lake where we might get help or a tow," she recalled. So Cindy jumped into the frigid water.

"I must have swum that boat for about twenty minutes until we got into the lake," she said. "Then I decided to give the engine one last try. I stayed in the water while my partner turned the key—and miraculously, the engine started.

"I told my partner to get that boat moving and no matter what, 'Don't let the engine die.' She was worried about my being in the water and wanted to help me back into the boat. But I told her to keep the boat moving slowly out into the lake while I tried to climb in. Getting into a boat from the water can be tough under the best of circumstances, but to do it while the boat is moving is really a test."

And Cindy flunked it. She eventually got one leg in the boat but that was the best she could do. Nevertheless, she wouldn't let her partner stop the boat or abandon the throttle because she was afraid the engine would die. Cindy was determined to get her two bass to the weigh-in on time.

"So that's how we headed back—with me half in and half out of the boat," she said. "We actually got back at 3 P.M. and I wasn't due at the weigh-in until 3:15. The officials told me to wait. But by then I was so wet, so cold, and so frozen that I yelled my head off that I had to weigh those fish now or freeze to death."

The officials relented, and it's a good thing they did. Right after Cindy recorded her fish, she was taken to the hospital where she was treated for hypothermia (dangerously low body temperature).

"Everybody thought I was crazy to jump into that freezing water and risk my life for two little bass," said Cindy. "But they were important fish. I finished in the Top 10 in that tournament. To me, that swim was worth it."

A True Sportsman

In 1991, Bob Crupi caught the second-biggest largemouth bass of all time—and then deliberately let it go!

Crupi ignored the financial benefits of landing a twenty-two-pound bass that was just a few ounces short of the most sought-after record in all of fishing. Rather than make money from displaying the trophy fish or doing endorsements, Crupi let the bass survive in his live well while he took it in for weighing, measuring, and photographing.

Then, in one of the most unselfish gestures in sport fishing, Crupi released the bass unharmed back into California's Castaic Lake.

Today, according to veteran anglers, that bass probably has grown larger than the twenty-two-pound, four-ounce world record set in 1932. Anyone who catches the largemouth is almost guaranteed a million dollars from endorsements, personal appearances, and other perks.

But none of that matters to Crupi. "I'm not in this for fame or money," he said. "This is a personal achievement. Among the guys I fish with, it's a pat on the back in recognition. I don't want endorsements. I'm not calling companies.

"I just want to go on and catch more big bass," added Crupi, who once anchored a seventy-two-pound, five-bass limit with a twenty-one-pounder.

When Crupi netted his twenty-two-pound bass, he was using live crayfish for bait. He knew the fish was close to the world record and raced back to shore with it in his live well. He then loaded his boat on a trailer and took the fish to a nearby market where it was weighed. The fish hit 22.01 on the scale, and was twenty-nine and a half inches long with a girth of twenty-seven and a half inches.

Crupi had pictures taken of him holding the fish before he put it back in his live well and sped back to Castaic, where he gently released the monster largemouth.

Unfortunately, the state of California has refused to recognize his fish as a new state record, because he released it before a state biologist could examine it.

But fishermen everywhere appreciate Crupi's ultimate act of catch-and-release . . . because now there's a million-dollar fish swimming out there for somebody to catch.

Fish Crazy

When Nate Berg was eleven years old, he decided he really loved to fish. So he made fishing a daily ritual for over three years.

Neither rain, nor sleet, nor snow—not even sickness—kept him from casting a line out every day. In fact, the incredible youth from Blair, Wisconsin, fished every single day for 1,262 straight days!

Although official records of such a feat aren't kept, fishing authorities don't know of anyone who can document a longer fishing streak.

"I just love to fish," said Nate, whose angling record earned him a letter from President George Bush, two appearances on *NBC Nightly News*, and a spot on Babe Winkleman's television fishing show.

Nate began his daily fishing routine on March 27, 1988, and kept it going from grade school into junior high. The toughest time for him was the winter. He once ice-fished in weather that had a windchill factor of sixty degrees below zero. Despite the frigid conditions, he still managed to land two perch.

Nate's record was in jeopardy one winter day when he woke up feeling sick and noticed the temperature outside was only twenty degrees. "I had gotten a lot of crappies the day before," he said, "So even though I felt bad, I went ice-fishing anyway."

Almost all his fishing was done on nearby Lake Henry. The Blair Community Center kept a running total of his consecutive fishing days on a community bulletin board and a local bank also featured his daily streak on its sign.

Nate's biggest fish during his long run was a ten-pound, eight-ounce carp. He also landed a thirty-one-inch northern pike and a twenty-one-inch largemouth bass.

"We knew where Nate was every day, and we knew he wasn't in trouble," said his proud parents, John and Kathy Berg. "He's a healthy kid."

The string of fishing days finally came to an end on September 9, 1991. And it was all because of football. Nate played end and defensive tackle for his junior high football team, which had a game starting at 6 P.M. that day. With school all day and the game in the evening, Nate just couldn't find the time to squeeze in some fishing.

So Nate started another streak the next day.

Born to Fish

British angler Jeremy Gunningham used his fishing gear for an "infantile" purpose—to help deliver his baby son!

At 4:15 A.M. one morning in 1992, his wife Debbie unexpectedly went into labor. Gunningham frantically called the doctor, but Debbie yelled from the bathroom that it was too late. Gunningham put down the phone and rushed to the bathroom, where he found that his wife had already delivered their son. However, Debbie was badly in need of some quick medical attention.

After cutting the umbilical cord, Gunningham needed to clamp it, and the only thing he could think of was a fish-hook remover he kept in his tackle box.

"I grabbed the only tools I knew how to use properly—my fishing gear," he said. The hook remover, which had a strong clamp on one end, worked just fine on the umbilical cord.

When the doctor arrived and needed more light to treat Debbie and the baby, Gunningham had just the thing—his fishing hat. "It has a miner's light on the front of it and I use it for night fishing," he explained. "It worked fine for the doctor."

Thanks to Gunningham's fishing gear, his wife and baby were in excellent condition. Said Debbie later, "Not many babies arrive with the help of a fishing hat and a hook remover."

The Great Emancipator

In seventy-seven days of fishing, David Romeo of East Meadow, New York, caught over 3,000 largemouth bass—and let all but twenty-four of them go free.

His unique feat earned him a spot in *The Guinness Book of World Records* for "most fish caught in a season." From April 1 to October 31, 1984, Romeo caught 3,001 bass on rod and reel in the fresh waters of Long Island.

The angler threw almost all of them back because, he said, he just enjoyed catching fish more than eating them.

At the beginning of the fishing season, the twenty-six-year-old tax consultant set a goal of landing 1,000 fish by the end of October. Fishing on weekends and on vacations, Romeo reached that mark on July 24. So he reset his goal at 2,000 fish, and attained that number by September 2. Then the angler went for broke—a never-before-attained 3,000.

With two days left in the season, Romeo was 109 fish short of his goal. So he spent the final weekend at one of his favorite fishing holes, Kahlers Pond in East Moriches (where he earlier had landed ninety-nine bass) and had his second-best day ever by snagging ninety-three on Saturday. The following morning—the last day of the season—the angler caught seventeen fish to better by one the magic number of 3,000.

Romeo said he embarked on his fishing odyssey to help conservationists by measuring each bass and recording the data in detailed log books.

"It was fun," said Romeo. "There was one fish with a deformed gill that was probably glad the season was over. I landed it six times."

The "Thill" of Victory

Mick Thill, the first American ever to win a medal in international freshwater fishing competition, once dazzled a competitor by catching 100 catfish—in twenty-one minutes!

"I told him that I could catch 100 catfish in twenty minutes, but I hadn't counted on getting stuck so badly by catfish spines when I was unhooking them," Thill said, explaining why he missed his goal by a single minute.

But it was still an amazing performance that left veteran fishermen in awe.

Thill was demonstrating his fishing method—using a long pole with a special ultra-light Thill float—at a Dallas tackle show in 1986, when he was challenged by a man who worked for a bait company. The man claimed no one could out-fish his system, which involved an ultra-light rod and reel, a small red and white round float, a two-pound-test line, and maggots for bait.

"I'll beat you," Thill responded and accepted an invitation to meet his challenger at a lake near Claremore, Oklahoma.

Before they started fishing, Thill chummed the area to see what was around and realized the place was full of small five- to eight-ounce channel catfish. That's when he boasted he could catch 100 in twenty minutes.

"I caught forty in the first ten minutes, then

started catching as many as ten fish a minute," said Thill. "The catfish were just boiling in the water over the maggot chum I was using."

Then the catfish spines began taking their toll. "On four or five occasions, the spine was embedded in my hand and I had to shake the catfish off," said Thill. "But I was so focused, I didn't feel a thing."

Needless to say, his stunned competitor was duly impressed— even though it took Thill an extra minute to catch his 100 fish.

Casting Call

Can a fisherman cast a golf ball farther than a golfer can hit it? Angler Steve Rajeff and PGA pro Fred Couples answered that question in a unique challenge.

Pulling out his trusty driver, Couples walloped the ball an impressive 333 yards.

Rajeff, longtime American casting champion in both distance and accuracy events, used a twelve-foot, two-handed surf rod with a revolving spool reel. The golf ball, which weighs a little less than two ounces, was attached to his line by a twenty-five-pound test mono leader. He then started swinging his rod around his head and let the ball fly—for a staggering 337 yards!

The angler had beaten the golfer by four yards.

A Can of Worms
Unlucky Experiences of Anglers

Too Much of a Good Thing

Angler Juhani Harju lost a major fishing tournament—because he caught too many fish!

Harju, of Finland, was vying at the 1985 Finnish National Ice Fishing Championships, an event in Finland comparable to the World Series in America. More than 5,000 fishermen competed in the event on huge Lake Pielisjarvi.

Under the rules, every fisherman stands on the shoreline and waits for the starting gun. Each angler then runs to the first spot where he wants to fish, hand-drills a hole, and then waits. Thirty minutes after the start, the fishing begins. Each competitor can fish as many holes as he wants, but must be back across the finish line with all his fish exactly three hours later. The event is both strenuous and frantic because fishermen run everywhere on the lake and drill new holes each time they relocate.

Harju was having a great day, pulling in dozens and dozens of perch. He didn't want to quit, but time was running out. Landing thirteen pounds of perch, the angler felt confident he was going to win the championship.

But Harju's good luck was also his bad luck. He had spent so much time catching fish that he had only a few minutes left to run the two miles back to the finish line. With his string of fish plus his gear and heavy winter clothing, the angler began staggering.

His catch seemed to get heavier with each step. Every muscle in his body was aching and his breathing was labored. Finally, the finish line was in reach. But with just twenty yards to go, the staggering angler collapsed, too spent to even crawl the rest of the way. Spectators

thought Harju had suffered a heart attack, but a quick examination found he had simply collapsed from physical exhaustion.

Instead of winning the championship—which would have meant valuable endorsements in Finland—Harju didn't even finish. He lost, even though his catch weighed two pounds more than the winner's.

Hat's Incredible

Bob Wofford's lucky hat wasn't so lucky. It cost him over $20,000 in prize money at a fishing tournament.

Wofford, forty, was fishing in his first bass event, the Texas Bass Championship on Lake Conroe, Texas, in 1992 when he landed a 7.64-pound largemouth bass. He was thrilled that the big fish wound up finishing fourth in the two-day tourney. He was even happier when he learned that he had won a prize for the largest fish of the hour. His total winnings, he was told, were $20,786.

But there was a catch to his catch.

"Where's your official tournament cap, the one you were given at registration?" tournament officials asked Wofford.

"Back on the dash of my partner's pickup truck," the puzzled angler replied. He had dumped the official tournament cap for his old lime-green "lucky" hat instead.

"Too bad," said tournament officials. "The rules state you must wear the tournament cap. You're disqualified. No prize, no cash."

Said a dejected Wofford later, "They cut me off at the knees and left me bleeding."

Honey-Marooned

A midwestern honeymoon couple chucked fishing and their clothes to fulfill a fantasy. But they ended up feeling like fish out of water.

Several years ago in the Florida Keys, fishing guide Randy Wayne White was hired by the couple for what he thought was going to be a fishing trip. Instead, as soon as White's back-country skiff cleared the marina, the husband whispered to the guide, "We don't really want to fish. Just drop us off on a deserted island and leave us alone for a couple of hours. It's always been a dream of ours."

When White returned a few hours later, he found the dream had turned into a nightmare for the couple.

While the coosome twosome were making love on the island, they failed to notice that the tide had come in and washed away all their clothes. They were left totally nude in the hot Florida sun.

White had no extra clothes on board and wasn't about to give up his shorts. So the guide helped the embarrassed, naked honeymooners into the boat and, while they crouched down low, took them back to the marina.

A Fine Kettle of Fish

The largest fishing fine ever paid was a whopping $2 million.

The fine was levied in 1985 against the giant Japanese fishing company, Nichiro Gyogyo Kaishi, whose twenty-one-ship fishing fleet was accused of under-reporting its catch off the Alaskan coast in 1982 and 1983.

The company agreed to pay the record fine and to forfeit its fishing permit in Alaskan waters for several years in return for the U.S. Justice Department's promise to drop a civil suit.

Well, Exc-u-u-u-se Me!

Northwest Wisconsin conservation warden Dave Swendsen has heard dozens of wacky excuses from anglers caught without their fishing license. Among the nuttiest are:

- "My license was in my pocket up until yesterday. But I lost it then when I fell overboard."
- "I had so much money in my billfold that I had to leave the license back in my cabin."

• "Actually, I'm not fishing. I'm just feeding the fish some worms."

• An angler trying to unwrap his plug and line from around his legs: "I wasn't fishing. I was swimming and I got tangled up with this line."

Beer Down

One brutally hot summer day, New York State Environmental Conservation Officer Donald Malmrose was on patrol on Chautauqua Lake when he approached a boat anchored offshore.

Its occupant was reclining in his seat and had a fishing pole hanging over the side. Recalled Malmrose, "I pulled alongside and asked to see his fishing license. He told me, 'I don't have one, but that's okay, because I'm not fishing.'"

"I said, 'If you're not fishing, then what's that line doing in the water?'"

"He then reeled up his line—and attached to it were three bottles of beer. 'I'm just cooling my beer,' he replied. 'Would you like one?'"

"I said, 'No, thanks,' laughed, and continued on patrol."

The Grand Lake Stream Kill

Thousands of salmon fry were needlessly killed in Maine's Grand Lake Stream in 1981—because a dam was closed solely to let two anglers retrieve their lost fishing rods!

State regional biologist Ron Brokaw said two New Yorkers were fishing in the stream in fast-flowing water near a Georgia-Pacific dam when somehow they lost their poles. Even though the stream was a natural landlocked salmon reproduction area, the two convinced the operator to close the dam, thus draining the immediate area of much of the water so they could find their rods.

The dam was closed for an hour, sharply reducing the water available to the stream, which was full of inch-long salmon. The fry, which were laid as eggs by native salmon weeks earlier, had just emerged from the bottom of their gravel bed nursery when their habitat was dried up. Fortunately, the adult salmon survived by swimming to an area where there was enough water.

"It's inconceivable that someone made a decision to shut down that dam for two fishing rods," fumed Brokaw. "Losing rods is just part of the fishing game."

Fish Strikes (Back)

Bizarre Injuries Inflicted by Fish

Paying for the Bill

In separate life-threatening ordeals, two fishermen were speared clean through their chests by the razor-sharp bills of giant marlins.

In 1989, Colin Mizuguchi, a twenty-eight-year-old hospital dietary assistant in Honolulu, was fishing with his friends off the Hawaiian coast when one of them hooked a six-foot marlin. After a thirty-minute fight, the fish was reeled to the side of the boat, where Mizuguchi tried to gaff it.

"Suddenly, it dived under the boat and swam behind us," he recalled. "Then, as I stood watching, the fish turned and charged straight at me. About ten feet from the back of the boat, the fish leaped, and flew through the air.

"It rammed into me with the force of a runaway train and its bill drove through my chest like a bayonet." The impact smashed Mizuguchi backward, and when he fell, the bill came out, leaving a massive, bleeding hole in his chest.

His friends rushed Mizuguchi back to shore where he received emergency treatment at the hospital. "The marlin's bill had narrowly missed my heart, gone right through my lung, and had broken a rib in my back," he said. "But miraculously, it didn't kill me."

Incredibly, three years later, another angler was impaled by a marlin in an almost identical accident.

In 1992, Australian Robert Breden, seventeen, was fishing with his pals off the coast near Melbourne when he tried to gaff a hooked 300-pound marlin. "As I looked down at the fish, I noticed his two-foot-long bill was pointed straight up at me," Breden recalled.

Suddenly, the marlin shot up out of the water, gored the teen-ager through the chest, then splashed back into the ocean.

At first the stunned youth didn't realize how badly he was hurt. Breden turned to his horrified fishing companions and asked, "Why am I bleeding from the back?" They told him the fish's bill had speared him through the chest.

Breden was rushed back to the dock and whisked to the hospital. In an amazing stroke of luck, the marlin's bill missed all of Breden's vital organs. The angler was treated for his wound and released.

Fishing's Strangest Death

In the most bizarre fishing death of all time, an angler was killed by a little five-inch bluegill!

Donald Lough, forty, of Paris, Ohio, was fishing with his wife on the banks of Tharmon Lake in nearby Robertsville in 1983 when he caught a bluegill. Lough then jokingly dangled it above his mouth as if he were going to swallow it.

But the fish slipped from his fingers and fell headfirst into the angler's open mouth. Tragically, the bluegill became lodged in Lough's throat, completely blocking his airway. The fisherman began choking but neither he nor his wife could pull out the bluegill.

His wife then frantically called paramedics, but by the time they arrived, it was too late. Lough had died. The bluegill was stuck so deeply in the angler's throat that the paramedics removed it only with the help of surgical pliers.

The Fish That Caught the Fisherman

Spearfisherman Ronnie Pace, a scuba diving instructor from Hattiesburg, Mississippi, was killed by a grouper who dragged him to his death.

While underwater near an oil rig off the coast of Louisiana in 1988, Pace shot his spear at what fellow scuba divers said was a giant 300-pound grouper. Suddenly, Pace and the fish disappeared into the depths.

Days later, Pace's body was found floating in the water. Authorities believe that Pace's spear line apparently wrapped around his arm when he shot the fish. The speared but still-powerful grouper then dragged Pace until the scuba diver ran out of air and died.

The Tarpon That Went Overboard

A free-jumping, 100-pound tarpon leaped into the boat of two startled fishermen, knocking one of them overboard and then causing $1,000 damage to their gear.

In 1992, David Rocque and his brother Marc of Melbourne, Florida, were fishing off the tip of Cape Canaveral when the six-foot unhooked tarpon suddenly soared into their twenty-two-foot boat. "I heard it come out of the water and all I had time to do was scream," said the angler. "It hit me square in the chest hard enough to knock me clear out of the boat."

Meanwhile, the tarpon began thrashing about the boat, breaking six fishing poles and a rodholder. When the fish finally got tired, David climbed back into the boat and he and his brother let it go free.

A Cat(Fish) Lover at Heart

Mitchell Lee Franklin tried to play catch with a catfish—and almost died as a result.

The strange, near-fatal incident occurred in 1992 when Franklin, of Chandler, Indiana, was fishing with his buddy, John Bullington, who had predicted that they weren't going to catch anything. Moments later, Franklin pulled a five-pound catfish out of a local creek.

Franklin unhooked the spiny catfish and playfully tossed it to his pal. Bullington carefully caught it without getting pricked and then, in lighthearted retaliation, threw it back at Franklin. Unfortunately, Franklin had just turned his head and didn't see the fish flying his way.

In a freak accident, the long spine on the back of the catfish stuck squarely—and deeply—into Franklin's chest. The pain was so intense that he nearly passed out.

"I looked down and saw the fish and thought it had stuck all the way down to my heart," recalled Franklin, who was rushed to the hospital. There, doctors found that the angler's heart was not injured, but the catfish spine had punctured his lung. The angler spent five days recovering from a collapsed lung and from the poisonous effects of the toxic slime on the catfish's spine.

The catfish, meanwhile, was filleted.

Fly Fishermen

Here was a 1984 tip to anglers from *Wisconsin Natural Resources* magazine: "Relieve yourself ashore—almost half of Wisconsin's boating fatalities are found with their flies open."

Snake-Bitten Angler

A fish avenged its own death!

One memorable day in 1984, Mark Parker, of Linton, Louisiana, caught a two-pound largemouth bass. He took it home, put it on a table, and began to clean it. Even though the fish was dead, it still managed to get its revenge.

As Parker stuck his finger in the bass's mouth, the angler was suddenly bitten by a snake! Only then did Parker discover that just before he had caught the bass, it had swallowed a foot-long, poisonous water moccasin. The snake was still alive inside the bass! When Parker had started to clean the bass, the snake slithered out of the fish's mouth and attacked the angler.

Parker killed the snake and then had to spend the night in the hospital recovering from the bite.

Killer Fishing Trip

Fishermen have died on the ocean, but only the four-man crew aboard the fishing trawler *Sunmore* had the dubious distinction of perishing from the highest wave ever recorded—over 1,700 feet high!

The killer wave roared down an Alaskan inlet known as Lituya Bay, near Juneau, on July 9, 1958.

During daylight hours the inlet was frequented by ocean liners, tour boats, and small fishing vessels. But on this fateful night, only the *Sunmore* was riding peacefully at anchor. Suddenly, earth tremors triggered a massive avalanche near Juneau—ninety million tons of rock and ice broke loose from a 3,000-foot-high precipice and came plunging down in a single mass at the very end of the inlet. It was like dropping a sack of cement into a bathtub.

The resulting wave roared down Lituya Bay at more than 100 miles per hour. Every tree and shrub growing on the sides of the inlet from sea level to as high as 1,720 feet was washed down the bay. The crew of the *Sunmore* had no warning . . . and no chance. In an instant, the boat was smashed to smithereens and the fishermen were pitched to a watery grave—victims of the highest wave in the recorded history of the ocean.

Knocked (Tr)out

A high school teacher who was extolling the virtues of fishing while on a field trip with his students was mugged—by a fish!

One day in 1991, Giovanni Bocchicchio, a ninth grade teacher in Italy, took his class to a neighborhood pond. "I was talking to them about the fun of fishing and the importance of keeping the environment clean," recalled Bocchicchio. "I was pointing to some litter at the edge of the pond, when suddenly the lights went out."

The students reported that as their teacher reached to retrieve a Styrofoam cup that had been thrown in the pond, a large trout suddenly leaped out of the water and smashed him in the jaw. And knocked him out!

"When I came to, the students were all just staring at me and the trout was flopping around on the ground," said Bocchicchio. "That's not the way I want to catch a fish."

Catch of the Dazed
The Strangest Trophies Ever Reeled In

A Reel Lifesaver

For a French fisherman, it truly was the catch of a lifetime. With his trusty rod and reel, he snagged a drowning woman and saved her life!

"I've dreamed all my life of the catch to beat them all. Well, this was it," said Francis Ardoin, who hooked a 170-pound woman after she tried to commit suicide by throwing herself into a canal.

He was using just six-pound test line at the time, yet he expertly reeled the unconscious woman to shore. The bizarre rescue occurred on March 31, 1991, as Ardoin stood on the bank of a canal near his home in Verdun-sur-Meuse, France. He was trying out a new rod and reel that his children had bought him, when he saw a woman float by in the canal.

"It was obvious she was about to drown," the fifty-six-year-old retired railroad worker recalled. "With one quick, smooth cast, I hooked her clothes. If it had been a fishing tournament, I'd never have been lucky enough to manage such an expert cast the first time."

His new rod nearly bent over under the weight of the water-logged woman, but the six-pound line held. Unfortunately, the new rod didn't. "Suddenly there was an ear-splitting 'CR-A-A-A-CK' and my rod snapped in two," Ardoin said. But he grabbed the line, pulled the woman closer to shore, then waded out the last few feet and carried her to the bank. The woman was rushed to a hospital, where she made a full recovery.

"Her husband later called to thank me," said Ardoin. "He told me his wife regretted her act and was glad to be alive."

Marveled Verdun police spokesman Captain André Issard: "It was a one-in-a-million chance that Ardoin could hook her with his fishing line. But he did it!"

Thumbs Up

Bob Lindsey lost his thumb in a boating accident in 1991 on Wyoming's Flaming Gorge Reservoir. Then the unbelievable happened. Seven months later, he got his thumb back— when it was found in the belly of a trout!

Another angler had caught the trout and discovered the missing digit when he was filleting the fish. He turned the thumb over to the local sheriff's department, who wondered if they had a murder on their hands. When Lindsey heard about the found thumb, he called the authorities and said it was probably his. Sure enough, X-rays proved it was.

Lindsey keeps the thumb in a jar at home now.

The year before, angler Corene McCallson was fishing on the Mississippi River when she snagged and reeled up an artificial arm.

"I was sure there was a body down there of a handicapped person," said McCallson after she reported her unusual catch to the police. An investigation revealed that the artificial arm belonged to sixty-six-year-old Chuck Rollins, of Caledonia, Minnesota, who was still very much alive. He had lost his artificial arm while water-skiing in the same area ten months earlier.

Something's Fishy at City Hall

It's hard enough to catch a fish in the putrid Chicago River, but someone actually caught a fish in the basement of city hall!

In 1992, the Chicago River poured through a broken tunnel downtown, paralyzing much of the Loop. It flooded basements of buildings, parts of the subway system, an underground walkway between city hall and the state office building, and other areas.

Many fish were sucked through the tunnel into the basements, including a yellow perch which was caught in the subway and a gizzard shad captured by hand in the city hall complex.

Chicago residents were unfazed by the unusual municipal catch—they'd always known there was something fishy about city hall.

Double Your Pleasure

Anglers keep their own personal records of the biggest fish they've ever caught. But how many have landed their two biggest fish ever—at the same time and on the same single-hook rig?

That's what happened to D.T. Bruce of Jasper, Florida, when he went fishing with a guide on Lake Yale in north Florida in 1987. Fishing with a live shiner, Bruce's targets were sunshine bass and largemouth bass.

Suddenly, he had a strike on his shiner and leaned back to set the hook. He knew immediately he had a big one. After a challenging battle, Bruce reeled the fish to the boat and up came a four-and-a-half-pound sunshine bass, the biggest fish he had ever caught in his life.

But Bruce was in for an even happier surprise.

The angler noticed there was no sign of the hook. Upon further examination, he saw the line continue through the sunshine's gills and down into the water. So Bruce resumed reeling in the line—and up came a whopping eight-and-a-half-pound largemouth bass!

Now *this* was the biggest fish he had ever caught.

Apparently, the sunshine bass struck the shiner, which somehow had worked its way through the bass's gills. The sunshine then started swimming away, even though it was still on the line. That's when the largemouth struck the hook. Bruce had the incredible good luck of landing both fish because the sunshine was caught by the line going through its gills while the largemouth was hooked.

In another stroke of good fortune, the French consul on the island of Mauritius caught two sailfish at once.

Maurice Paturau's unique catch occurred in 1974 while trolling off the island. The first sailfish struck the trolled bait and was hooked. But then a second sailfish jumped across the line—and got tangled up in it.

Now Paturau was fighting two jumping sailfish on the same line—one hooked and one about 50 yards above the hook, held captive by a bizarre tangle of line.

Amazingly, Paturau landed both sailfish, which each weighed seventy-seven pounds.

Crazy Catches

• In 1976, John Bembers lost his wristwatch in the water while fishing in Lake Michigan. Three years later, it turned up inside the stomach of a forty-two-pound salmon caught by Thomas Kresnak of Grand Rapids, Michigan. Apparently, the salmon had scooped up the shiny watch, thinking it was food. Incredibly, the watch still worked!

• Gosselin Deleus lost his glasses off the English coast in 1988 when he leaned over the side of a boat and they fell into the sea. A month later, a Belgian fisherman found a pair of glasses in the belly of a monkfish caught off the Belgian coast. Deleus read about the catch in a fishing magazine and contacted the Belgian—and got his glasses back.

• Ivan Olson and Nick Hanuschewicz were fishing Sixmile Creek north of Madison, Wisconsin, in 1984 when they caught a thousand-pounder—a 750 cc Kawasaki motorcycle! They hauled the motorcycle out, then called police. The cycle had been reported stolen.

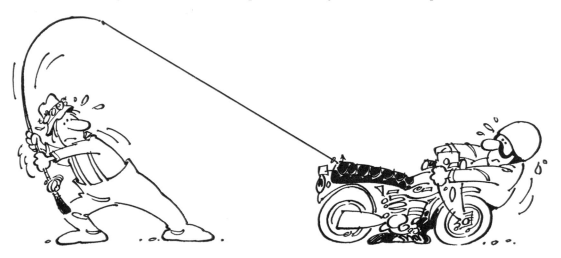

• In 1975, a fisherman's gill net in Lake Michigan, far from shore, pulled up a carriage, vintage 1850. Apparently, the carriage had been swept off a schooner during a storm more than 100 years earlier.

Kamikaze Kingfish

A thirty-pound king mackerel caught itself!

In 1992, Florida fishermen Brian Nash and Mike Harper were drifting in their twenty-two-foot boat off the coast of Fort Lauderdale, hoping to land a kingfish.

The anglers hadn't caught a thing all day, when suddenly the surface nearby bubbled with rainbow runners. Then out of the water leaped the kingfish, which had crashed the baitfish. "He came toward the boat like incoming artillery," said Harper.

"I was looking for a place to hide," added Nash, who took cover under the console. "I was thinking about jumping overboard. The fish was looking dead at us as he came in. He was in a definite panic."

The kingfish slammed into the console's windshield and shattered it, then landed in the back of the boat. "Plexiglas was everywhere," said Nash. "When he hit the deck, it sounded like a bomb going off."

The kingfish thrashed on the deck, snapping its jaws, whacking tackle boxes, and scattering fishing rods. Nash grabbed a baseball bat, but couldn't get a good swing at the fish.

"Brian couldn't even hit him because he was moving so much," said Harper. "The fish put about six dents in the bottom of the boat before he was subdued. We celebrated, high-fiving each other, when the fish came back to life and almost jumped out of the boat."

A few more swings of the bat ended the kingfish's comeback attempt for good. Then Harper and Nash surveyed the damage—a shattered $200 windshield—and counted their blessings.

Said Harper, "Thank God it wasn't a marlin."

A Dime's Worth of Fishing

In a one-in-a-million catch, fishing guide Ken Harris came up with a ten-cent bonus. In 1987, Harris, of Key West, Florida, took his out-of-state clients for a day of dolphin fishing. His anglers were impressed by the clarity of the water in the Florida Straits. To demonstrate how clear it was and how far down they could see, Harris tossed a dime overboard. As it floated down 60 feet, Harris remarked, "Watch a dolphin come along and hit the dime."

Amazingly, right on cue, a school of small dolphin appeared—and one of them actually swallowed the dime! The fishermen then grabbed their rods and began catching fish.

The anglers were still marveling at the dime-eating dolphin when they returned to Key West and began cleaning their catch. Incredibly, when they cut open one of the dolphin, they found the dime!

"What do you think the odds are against throwing a coin overboard in 700 feet of water and getting it back?" Harris asked. "I know I'm going to be telling that story and have people scoff at me for a long time."

Caught in the Act

According to British news accounts, English fisherman Mark Swinburne was convicted of assault after using his rod and reel to catch his wife cheating on him.

Police said that in 1990, Swinburne, thirty-one, of Wednesbury, England, suspected that his wife was seeing another man at their home. So the angler hooked his line to the bedroom curtains and patiently waited outside with his rod and reel in hand.

The report said that when Swinburne heard a male voice in the couple's bedroom, the angler reeled open the curtains and caught his wife in a clinch with another man.

According to the authorities, the outraged hubby threw down his rod, rushed into the house and attacked the twosome, who managed to call police. Swinburne was arrested and confessed to assaulting his wife and her beau. The angler was sentenced to six months in jail and fined $500 for his outrageous catch of the day.

Weigh to Win!
Incredible Performances in Tournaments

Seven-Eleven

Jack Chancellor cast his place in fishing history when, during the most prestigious of all bass fishing tournaments, he caught an incredible eleven bass—in just seven minutes!

It happened during the 1982 BASS Masters Classic on the Alabama River.

Chancellor was using a plastic worm he made called the "Do Nothing Worm" in open water eighteen feet deep when he got the first strike. He lost that fish, but then used another rod with a Jack's Jigging Spoon on it.

"I hadn't caught a fish all morning," recalled Chancellor, of Phenix City, Alabama. "Then at exactly seven minutes to noon I started catching bass so quick, I was just throwing them in the bottom of the boat." He reeled in eleven bass—each about one and a half pounds—in just seven minutes. Then, just as amazingly as it started, the fishing frenzy completely stopped.

"I've never before or since caught that many fish that fast in competition," said Chancellor. "Everything was gloom and doom, then all of a sudden, I had caught my limit and then some. You can imagine how that made me feel."

Those fish helped Chancellor place second in the Classic and win $12,000.

Top Cat

Pro angler Jerry Whitfield is so good at catching catfish that no one will compete against him.

Whitfield, of Hartwell, Georgia, holds the record for the biggest string of catfish ever caught in the Catfish Hall of Fame tournaments held at Randolph's Landing on Lake Marion, South Carolina. In two days of fishing, Whitfield brought in a record 279 pounds of catfish in the September 1989 event.

He also holds the record for the biggest catfish caught in the competition, a sixty-two-pounder.

Whitfield won the tournament so often that it was decided to set up a pro and an amateur division just to give amateur anglers a better chance.

But, said Rick Gray, who operates Randolph's Landing, Whitfield promptly made a shambles of the small pro field, and soon no one would enter that division. So the pro division was eliminated and the tournament now is open only to amateurs, which effectively shuts out Whitfield.

"He's the best I've ever seen," Gray said. "Everybody's afraid of him."

Beat the Clock

In one of competitive fishing's most dramatic finishes, pro bass fisherman Rob Kilby had time for only two more casts. Incredibly, he then landed two five-pound bass and returned to the weigh-in with less than a minute to spare.

Going into the last day of the 1990 Alabama Invitational at Lake Guntersville, Kilby knew that he needed twelve to fourteen pounds of bass to make the exclusive entry list for the upcoming BASS Masters Classic. At 2 P.M., with the weigh-in only thirty minutes away, he had only three small fish, totaling about three pounds, and it looked like he had failed in his bid to make the Classic.

"I remembered then what Larry Nixon [one of the all-time bass fishing greats] had told me the night before—that he had been catching fish on soft plastic lizards and he was fishing the points," recalled Kilby, of Hot Springs, Arkansas. "He even gave me some of his lures.

"I don't like to fish somebody else's way, but my way wasn't working. I ran to an area that resembled what he was talking about. I looked at my watch and realized I had no more than six or seven minutes to fish before I had to leave for the weigh-in.

"Then I got a strike. He was so big I almost had a heart attack getting him in. It was a five-pounder. 'Boy, if I could catch one more,' I thought.

"And then I did. On my second cast, I nailed another five-pounder. That gave me a total of thirteen pounds, just enough to make the Classic."

Kilby got back to the weigh-in with his fish with less than a minute remaining. Thanks to his remarkable, last-second effort, the angler qualified for the 1990 Classic, in which he finished third and won $10,000.

The Worst of the Best

After two and a half hours of the 1982 International Fishing Championships, not one of the world's thirty-seven best fishermen had caught a single fish!

In the final half hour of the three-hour tournament, held in Northern Ireland's Newry Canal, England's Kevin Ashurst caught eight small fish that totaled a measly one pound, seven and one-half ounces. Incredibly, the puny amount was enough to win the gold medal!

It was the lowest winning total ever in international competition.

Experts believe that the fish had simply been spooked in the canal because of the noise and commotion of the crowd watching the event.

The Magic Tree

Pro angler Chris Houston, one of Bass'n Gals' all-time money winners, has enjoyed plenty of fantastic fishing in her life. But the greatest—and strangest—was the thirty minutes she spent at "The Magic Tree."

During practice at the 1986 Bass'n Gal Invitational at Patoka Lake, Indiana, Chris and her husband, television fishing star Jimmy Houston, caught a couple of bass around a tree sticking up through twenty-five feet of water. But Chris did not fish the tree early in the tournament, leaving it for later.

On the final day, she went immediately to the tree and started casting a Zara Spook. Within a minute, a bass savagely struck the topwater plug. Chris cast again and quickly landed another bass. In less than thirty minutes, Chris had caught seven bass, the biggest about five pounds.

"It was amazing," she recalled. "What a moment. I kept fishing on and off at that tree all day—but I never got another bite after those first thirty minutes."

But her official five-fish, eighteen-pound string—all caught at what she dubbed "The Magic Tree"—enabled Chris to win the tournament.

Ironically, "The Magic Tree" was ignored by all the other anglers in the tourney—even though it was located only five minutes from the tournament launch point.

Whiz Kid

Veteran fishermen were put to shame at the second U.S. National Bank Matchfishing Championships at Crab Orchard Lake, Illinois, in 1992 when an eleven-year-old girl stole the show.

Felicia Breen, of Champaign, Illinois, won more than just the American Junior Championship for boys and girls nine to eleven years old. She also won the Ladies Overall Champion award and had the second highest poundage of any adult angler in the tournament.

Only one man beat her—and he was former world champion Mick Thill.

Felicia won both of her two three-hour fishing heats with a total catch of bluegills and channel cats that weighed twenty-six pounds, five ounces.

"She's amazing," said Thill. "She's a natural and super talented."

Child's Play

No youngsters ever dominated a fishing tournament like the Hartman brothers did on Crystal Lake, Illinois, in 1989. They caught more fish than all the other 118 competitors combined!

Tim Hartman, fourteen, and his brother Jim, twelve, had only two hours of introduction to tournament bank fishing when they entered their first contest, the Crystal Lake Junior Team Fishing Championships.

However, in just two hours, the pair caught 159 bluegills, crappie, and sunfish—more fish than all the other 118 kids participating combined. Tim caught eighty-four and Jim seventy-five.

In 1992, three years later, Jim went on to win the American Junior Pro Championship for ages thirteen through eighteen, at Crab Orchard Lake, Illinois.

Cash Crappie

Even though crappie tournaments typically pay no more than $2,000 or $3,000 for first place, pro angler Sam Shealy once won more than $107,000 in just two days of crappie fishing.

"He's our biggest winner of all time," said Tony Estes, president of the organization that runs crappie tournaments throughout the country.

Shealy, of Newhill, North Carolina, is not only a top crappie catcher but a remarkably lucky one. In Crappiethon USA tournaments, the winner nets a relatively small amount of cash—unless he catches a certain tagged fish while using a specific sponsor's fishing gear or supplies. Then his payday can soar by tens of thousands of dollars just for landing one fish.

That's what happened to Shealy, when in two days of fishing he earned more than $100,000 in bonus money.

In 1991 Shealy hooked a tagged crappie that turned into a $40,000 fish because at the time he was using the right sponsor's product—a Crab Claw anchor. Then the following year, on Lake Okeechobee in Florida, Shealy caught a fish worth $65,000 because he was using the right Johnson spinning outfit. He added another $2,110 for winning the tourney.

Two days of fishing brought Shealy a total of $107,110. "Not bad for a tournament fee investment of only a few hundred dollars," said Crappiethon USA's Tony Estes.

Two-Bass Hit

One cast for bass pro Greg Hines earned him $53,000—when two big bass hit the plug at the same time.

"It was the biggest payday of my career," the Arizona fisherman said about his most memorable fishing experience, which occurred on the third day of the 1981 U.S. Open on Lake Mead.

Hines, who was in first place at the time, was two fish short of his limit when he cast his Zara Spook towards a likely looking spot. Wham! . . . a bass hit the surface plug on top. Then, to the angler's astonishment, a second bass tried to take the plug away from the first fish!

"When I set the hook, I knew I had a decent fish," he recalled. "But then a tad later, it felt really big. I soon saw I had two fish on and both were nice bass. I didn't think I could get both of them in. I was sure one would pull the hook."

But Hines won his fight, landing two three-pound bass at the same time. The double catch fulfilled his limit and ensured his victory in the prestigious tournament.

"I've hooked two bass before on the same cast," said Hines, "but never two this big."

Minnow-Scule Victory Margin

No national fishing title was ever decided by a narrower margin than the 1991 Yamaha National Elite Angler Fish-off—when only a minuscule l/100th of an ounce separated the champion from the runner-up.

Walter "Bo" Boren of Green Cove Springs, Florida, reeled in five bass weighing 11.41 pounds from Sam Rayburn Lake in Texas. Runner-up Walter Owens brought in 11.40 pounds.

The 1/100th of an ounce meant $2,000 cash, a gold ring, and several Yamaha products for winner Boren, including a new ATV and motor.

Hooks, Lines, and Stinkers
Amazing Angling Facts

Raining Catfish and Dogs

Fish actually have rained down from the sky!

In full view of flabbergasted people—and duly reported in local newspapers around the globe—live fish have fallen from clouds onto streets and yards, sometimes miles from the nearest water. For example:

• During a storm in the city of Yoro in the mountains of Honduras in 1992, live sardines dropped from the sky by the thousands.

• In 1989, residents of Ipswich, Australia, thirty miles from the coast, were awakened by a tap-tap-tapping on their roofs. They were shocked to discover fish were raining down on their town. Squirming sardines were scooped up by the score that morning.

• In 1984, Pacific anchovies fell from clouds over the San Diego area.

Scientists theorize that on these rare occasions, storm updrafts—such as water spouts—over lakes, rivers, or oceans suck small fish up in the air, carry them for several miles, and then drop them like hail.

Men Stink

Men "stink" when it comes to fishing—and that's why women are better anglers. It's a scientific fact.

In 1951, two Canadian researchers conducted a study that found people give off a scent from an amino acid in the body called serine, which is detectable to fish.

Fish tend to shy away from serine, said the scientists, which is bad news for men because they have a lot of serine in their body. Women, on the other hand, have just a trace. The amount of serine varies from individual to individual, which may explain why one man will catch many more

fish than a male companion fishing the same way right next to him.

The scientists claim that when men put their hands or feet in the water or when they handle bait and put it into the water, they give off a warning odor. Once the fish detect this scent, they stay away. But the fish are less likely to avoid women anglers because females don't give off the odor.

A British scientist, Peter Behan, professor of clinical neurology at Glasgow University, has a different theory why women make better fishermen. His 176-page book, *Salmon and Women: The Feminine Angle*, argues that fish are attracted to female hormones.

"God meant for us to fish," boasts Sugar Ferris, president of Bass'n Gals, a women's fishing organization. "That's all there is to it."

The Mother of All Fishing

The very first fishing manual ever published was written by a woman nearly 500 years ago.

More than 150 years before Izaak Walton—the father of sport fishing—published his famous *The Compleat Angler*, Dame Juliana Berners, prioress of the Benedictine convent near St. Albans, England, hand-wrote *Treatise of Fishing with an Angle* in 1496.

It includes such time-tested advice as how to: construct a two-section rod, fish below waterfalls or in deep pools, fish when the wind is either from the south or west, and use a wire leader for pike.

Alluring Prices

A little three-inch-long copper and brass minnow lure fetched a whopping $22,000—the highest price ever paid for a piece of antique fishing gear.

The lure, made by Riley Haskell of Painesville, Ohio, in 1859, brought the record price at an auction in 1985.

"No one lure is definitely the most expensive in value," said Rich Treml of the National Fishing Lure Collectors Club. "Several, including the Heddon Handcarved Frog Lure from the 1890s, and the Flying Hellgrammite, the first wooden body lure which was made by the Comstock Lure Co. of New York in the 1880s, are near the top in value."

Eighty percent of old lures are worth $20 or less, Treml said. Only about fifty of the tens of thousands of such lures are worth $1,000 or more. Other antique fishing gear can fetch big bucks, too. A brass fishing reel made in 1810 by George Snyder of Kentucky fetched $20,000.

Not all valuable tackle comes from the 1800s. A six-foot-long bamboo trout rod made by Pinky Gillum of Connecticut in the 1940s recently sold for $19,200.

"Pinky Gillum was probably the best rodmaker there ever was," said Greg Hamilton, a fishing tackle consultant for the Oliver Gallery, an auction house in Kennebunk, Maine. "The second best rodmaker was Jim Payne from New York. He made short bamboo trout rods from the 1920s to the 1950s. Good ones can fetch $4,000 to $6,000."

Hooked on Lures

Dr. R.I. Hartzell has assembled one of the world's unique collection of lures. Some are pretty, others old, and a few hand-carved. But what sets his collection apart from all others is that every lure was once embedded in a part of a fisherman's anatomy.

Hartzell, a rural physician from Grantsburg, Wisconsin, has been extracting lures from anglers' thumbs, ears, and feet for over forty years. And whenever possible, he keeps the lures to add to his collection.

"I tried to con as many people out of their baits as I could," said Hartzell. "At the time, the bait is their enemy. So before they think about it, they'll let you have their bait. It got to be a little game to see if I could talk them out of their bait."

Hartzell didn't get them all, but his collection of hooks and lures numbered 310 when he donated it to the National Fresh Water Fishing Hall of Fame in Hayward, Wisconsin. Hartzell figured he has removed about 600 hooks since he set up his practice in Grantsburg in 1949.

"Most of the time, getting stuck happened because of carelessness by their partner in the boat," said Hartzell. "Sometimes it was from the fish in the boat jumping around. I've had at least a dozen people come in with hooks in more than one finger and I've had the same fisherman in here more than once."

Hartzell has extracted hooks from anglers when it wasn't even fishing season. "I've had a couple of people who got a hook in their fingers just by cleaning out their tackle box in the middle of winter," he said.

Fishing Poll

Here's a surprise: Anglers don't go fishing to catch fish! They don't even care that much about eating them!

According to a survey by the American Fishing Tackle Manufacturers Association, catching a lot of fish ranks near the bottom of reasons why anglers go fishing.

The main reason to take up the sport, said most fishermen, was to enjoy the outdoors.

Here are the survey results of why anglers fish:
- To enjoy the outdoors 49%
- To forget about problems 34%
- To spend time with the family 29%
- To have fun, even without catching a fish 29%
- To spend time alone 24%
- To be in the company of friends 17%
- To use skills to catch a difficult fish 12%
- To catch a lot of fish 7%
- To have fish for dinner 6%

Fish Tales

The World's Most Incredible Fish

The Catfish Are Biting

Eleven-year-old Tommy Stanton was water-skiing on Lake Eufaula in Oklahoma in 1985 when he suddenly vanished beneath the surface. He bobbed up just long enough to scream, "Daddy, he's got me!" Then Tommy went under again.

His terrified father leaped overboard and rescued his son from the jaws of an underwater menace—a giant catfish!

"There was a mouthprint all the way down Tommy's leg from knee to ankle," recalled his mother, Barbara Stanton.

The huge catfish got away. Fortunately, Tommy was not hurt.

It could have been worse. There have been reports of giant catfish attacking and eating children who were swimming or fishing in the wrong place at the wrong time.

In Europe, the remains of young children have been found in the stomachs of giant Wels Catfish—fish that have reached lengths of sixteen feet and weights of over 400 pounds. However, biologists believe the human remains were probably the result of the giant catfishes' scavenging of youngsters who already had drowned.

There are no 400-pound catfish in American waters. The largest ever caught officially on hook and line was "only" 110 pounds.

The Love Connection

When fish went on a rampage and started biting people in Lake Mendocino, California, people blamed the mysterious attacks on everything from piranhas to evil spirits—until scientists determined the culprits were sex-starved catfish!

Six different biting incidents in a two-week period in 1988 virtually closed the lake down. Three of the victims required medical attention.

Finally, experts went to investigate. "There is something unusual going on here," Weldon Jones, a state biologist, said at the time. "Generally, fish don't attack people."

Piranhas—the toothy, meat-eating South American fish—were immediately blamed. But after extensive netting of the lake, not a single piranha was found.

What were found, however, were large numbers of catfish in heat—and a decided lack of food for them. Catfish are known to be feisty when sexually aroused, hungry, or hassled, said Jones.

And the Lake Mendocino catfish were both aroused and hungry—and took it out on any human leg they could chomp on. The attack of the catfish was finally over when the spawning season ended.

Jail Bait

The county attorney in Niagara County, New York, actually ordered a fifteen-and-one-half-pound rainbow trout held in the county jail—for two years.

The fish hadn't done anything wrong, but it was the key evidence in a trial that took two years to resolve. So the trout was kept in the jail freezer all that time.

In the bizarre case, the trout appeared to be the winning fish in the 1981 Niagara County Trout and Salmon Derby. But the county attorney saw a spot near the gill that he felt was a puncture mark—meaning the fish might have been illegally snagged. He ruled against the fisherman who had entered the big trout.

The fisherman brought a taxidermist to court who testified that his examination of the fish showed it had been caught fairly and legally—and the jury believed him. In 1983, the fisherman was finally awarded his first-place prize of a boat, motor, trailer, and other winnings that totaled $25,000.

Walleyed Walleye

A walleye tried a sneak attack on a shad—but wound up getting its teeth knocked out instead.

Walleye were crashing shad all around Allan Byers on Lake Shelbyville in Illinois in 1985 when a seven-pounder zeroed in on a shad and launched a brutal surprise attack—and missed.

The fish ran smack into a log and literally knocked itself silly. Byers picked up the stunned walleye floating on the surface and discovered it had knocked its front teeth out and was still bleeding from the impact.

Not that it mattered—Byers knew what to do with the tasty fish. He took it home and ate it.

The Monster of Okanagan Lake

An underwater monster lurks in a Canadian lake!

While fishing in 1989, Ken Chaplin and his dad spotted a strange, gigantic water creature and captured it on videotape. The Canadian government was so impressed with their film that it put the monster on its protected wildlife list.

Ken's dad first spotted a strange lizard-like creature with a long neck and tail while fishing from the shore of sixty-mile-long Okanagan Lake in British Columbia, Canada. When

Ken learned about the sighting, he went to the lake with his video camera armed and ready. The water beast failed to show.

But Ken didn't give up. He returned the next day and, to his surprise, saw the creature and videotaped it. The beast, which Ken filmed over the next several days, appeared to be about fifteen feet long, had dark green and brown spots, and resembled a Loch Ness–type monster.

The locals began calling it "Ogopogo."

"I saw Ogopogo five evenings in a row, and caught it on video four separate times," said Ken, who put together a three-minute video on the creature and showed it to local politicians, wildlife experts, and government authorities.

"They came in skeptics and went out believers."

The biggest believer of all was the British Columbia government.

"Ogopogo now has the official protection of the government," said Jim Walker, director of the Wildlife Branch of British Columbia's Ministry of Environment. "An amendment to the Wildlife Act describes Ogopogo as an animal more than nine feet in length, not a sturgeon, and a resident in Okanagan Lake."

Still, nobody knows what it is or where it came from. Meanwhile, fishermen keep a wary eye out for Ogopogo—and wonder if good fortune or bad luck will follow the angler who catches him.

Hoi Polloi Koi

Most fishermen turn up their noses at the lowly carp—but a relative of the carp is the most expensive fish on the planet. It's worth as much as $200,000!

And that's not for winning a tournament. Japanese koi, which look like fancy goldfish but are in the carp family, go for big dollars to hobbyists who fancy the fish for its distinctive color and patterns.

Koi breeders display their champions at fish shows all over the globe. *The Guinness Book of World Records* lists the highest price ever paid for a champion koi as $131,783. But Takemi Adachi, owner of California Koi Farms Inc., in Fallbrook, California, said that some fish have been bought for between $200,000 and $250,000 in Japan.

No two koi have the same exact markings. The fish live to be hundreds of years old, can be fed by hand, grow to several feet long, and are raised all over the world.

One American koi breeder, Bob Fenner, owner of a koi firm in San Diego, says: "If you had a perfect koi—a large red and white fish with a pattern that looks like a perfect flower blossom—it would not surprise me if a wealthy Japanese collector paid up to $1 million for it."

Home Not So Sweet Home

"Tanglefree Tom," a two-pound crappie worth $50,000 to the angler who could catch it, ran out of luck at a 1988 Crappiethon USA tournament on Cumberland Lake in Kentucky.

For the seven years it took for Tom to reach two pounds, the crappie had not been hooked. But Tom finally was caught during a pre-tournament foray by event officials in a creek off the main lake. He was tagged with the "Tanglefree Tom" label that made him worth $50,000 to anyone catching the fish with the right Johnson spinning outfit. Then Tom was taken twenty-two miles away to the Cumberland Dam and released.

Two weeks later, during the tournament, angler Cecil Roy of Russell Springs, Kentucky, took his boat down that very same little creek where Tom was first caught—and landed him again! Because Roy was using the right Johnson spinning outfit, the catch netted him $50,000. Luckily for Roy, and unfortunately for Tom, the fish had determinedly swam twenty-two miles back from the dam to his home creek. But for Tom, "no place like home" meant the end of the line for him—caught twice in two weeks after years of freedom.

The Shark That Wanted to Be Caught

A shark was so dumb and so hungry that in less than an hour, it got hooked six times by anglers on the same boat!

In 1977, Mike Leech—now president of the International Game Fish Association—his wife Gussie, and his father were trolling with live yellowtail off the coast of Bimini when a dusky shark hit one of their baits. After a ten-minute fight, the six-and-a-half-foot shark was brought beside the boat.

Leech tagged the shark with the bright yellow tag from the National Fisheries Services and then let it swim away. The angler then re-rigged three fresh live baits, and five minutes later, he and his dad both got hits. "My dad and I grabbed the rods, and soon realized we were both fighting the same fish," Leech recalled. "After bringing it to the boat, we got a surprise. It was the same shark we had just released! It had swallowed both our fresh rigger baits."

Again, Leech cut the two leaders and watched the shark swim away. Out went three more live yellowtails.

"A few minutes later, we heard both riggers snap loose and again Dad and I grabbed the rods," said Leech. "You can imagine our amazement when, after a short battle, we brought the same shark alongside the boat and saw its yellow tag. That fish had swallowed both our rigger baits."

After the leaders were cut on the fourth and fifth hooks in the shark's jaw, the anglers sped out of the area before the shark could chomp on any more of their diminishing supply of live bait.

The anglers cruised to a spot about two miles away from their last encounter with the shark. A half hour later, they hooked a heavy fish and worked it up from about 100 feet deep. "When it came into sight,

I couldn't believe my eyes," said Leech. "There was the yellow tag protruding from the back of our friend, the shark!"

And for the sixth time, Leech cut the leader and released the shark. The anglers had seen enough of this persistent, dim-witted shark, so they switched to a bait that wasn't quite so appetizing. They rigged up some dead mullet and trolled away—and never saw the shark again.

Reel Crazy
Astonishing Records of Anglers

The Six-Second Man

The most fish ever caught in one hour by one man with one pole is a mind-boggling 590! That's almost one fish every six seconds!

Patrick Burckenstock, a twenty-eight-year-old Frenchman who specializes in speed fishing, set the world record in 1991 during a tournament on a small river in central France. He fished for the record in front of a group who timed his amazing exploit.

Burckenstock used a seven-foot pole with one-pound-test line and a Number 16 hook on it, with a red bead as bait. The fish he caught were abelettes, minnow-like fish from two to five inches long.

His secret was his chum. He mixed a special blend of finely ground bread, silkworm cocoons, oyster shells, sugar, powdered milk, and other ingredients. Then he spread the chum out on the water which got the fish in a feeding frenzy.

Burckenstock, who practices speed fishing five to six days a week, then averaged six seconds to hook an abelette, yank it out of the water, take if off the hook, and toss the line back in.

Bait Debate

Clive Green caught the largest fish ever landed by one man on rod and reel—but it didn't count because he used the wrong bait!

Green was fishing off Albany, Western Australia, on April 26, 1976, when he hooked a 3,388-pound great white shark. It easily bested the existing world record for the largest fish ever caught—also a great white, weighing 2,664 pounds and stretching over sixteen feet long, by Alf Dean in 1959 off the Australian coast.

But Green was using whale meat for bait, and that's a no-no in today's whale-sensitive world, so none of the ruling bodies of sportfishing count his catch as a true record. Dean's catch is considered the official mark.

Both landed sharks were dwarfed by the twenty-foot, four-inch great white harpooned by fishermen near Sao Miguel in the Azores. It weighed over 5,000 pounds!

The largest marine animal ever killed by one man was a ninety-seven-foot-long blue whale. Archer Davidson harpooned the whale by hand in New South Wales's Twofold Bay in 1910. Although the whale was never weighed, its tail flukes alone measured twenty feet across and its jawbone, twenty-three feet, four inches.

The largest freshwater fish ever caught on rod and reel was a 468-pound white sturgeon by Joey Pallotta on July 9, 1983, in the Carquinez Strait of California.

The Fisher Kings

When it comes to fishing, a handful of fishermen hold most of the top records. For instance:

• Mike Berg holds every National Fresh Water Fishing Hall of Fame (NFWFHF) fly-fishing record for gizzard shad, setting seven of the ten records on the same day—February 26, 1990—in the same place, Wolflake, Indiana.

• Rick Sanchez owns all the NFWFHF king salmon fly-fishing records, and all were set during five days of one vacation to Alaska's Talkeetna River in 1989.

• John Piper holds every bowfin on fly record, plus three garfish fly records, all caught at Blue Cypress Lake, Florida.

• Every NFWFHF arctic sheefish record is owned by an angler with the last name of Hudnall—twenty-one by Lawrence Hudnall and seven by his cousin, Dan Hudnall. Twenty-three of the twenty-eight records were set on Alaska's Kobuk River.

The Babe Ruth of Anglers

Lawrence Hudnall is the world record-holder of world records—owning an astonishing ninety-three different marks.

And almost as astounding as the number of records he holds is the variety of fish he's caught.

In a sampling of his incredible angling, Hudnall, a lumber yard manager from Dyer, Indiana, owns:

- 21 sheefish records
- 5 lake trout records
- 17 chum salmon records
- 4 steelhead records
- 12 pink salmon records
- 14 sockeye salmon records
- 3 coho salmon records, including two on the same day
- line class records for yellow perch, bowfin, burbot, grayling, Atlantic salmon, king salmon, cutthroat trout, and Dolly Varden trout.

Hudnall got started on his record-setting spree in 1984 when the Berkeley Line Co. came out with a program that offered $1,000 for any record set with its line.

"I was making my first trip to Alaska that year and every line class was open for several Arctic species, so I just went for it," Hudnall recalled.

He used to fish about 100 days a year, but now the father of four is limited to a once-a-month local outing and one major trip a year, usually to Alaska.

Of all his records, Hudnall said the mark that stands out the most for him is his eighty-six-pound all-tackle sheefish record.

Search for the Perch

Incredibly, the record that has stood the longest in the fishing world is for one of the most frequently caught fish—the yellow perch.

Dr. C.C. Abbot landed a four-pound, three-ounce yellow perch at Bordentown, New Jersey, in May, 1865. Despite the millions of yellow perch caught since, his record still stands as the largest perch ever caught.

Several other freshwater records have stood the test of time. Among them:

• A fourteen-pound, eight-ounce brook trout caught July, 1916
• A forty-one-pound cutthroat trout caught December, 1925
• A seventy-nine-pound, two-ounce Atlantic salmon caught 1928

Small Fry

The smallest fish that either the International Game Fish Association or the National Fresh Water Fishing Hall of Fame will recognize as any kind of line class or all-tackle record is only one pound. Yet, a surprising number of fish hold records at that minimum weight.

The smallest 1992 record-holding fish is the grass pickerel—a one-pounder holds the all-tackle record. If you catch a grass pickerel weighing more than one pound on any line test with any tackle, you could automatically become a world record holder.

Other one-pound records to try to best are:
• rock bass on two-pound-test line
• pumpkinseed sunfish on eight-pound-test line
• black bullhead in the "pole, no reel" class
• golden trout on sixteen-pound-test and all unlimited line class entries

The smallest saltwater record-holding fish is the one-pound, six-ounce striped burrfish. Other saltwater small fry are: two-pound, two-ounce flounder; two-pound lizardfish; one-pound, ten-ounce pinfish; and a two-pound, four-ounce sand tilefish.

Castmasters

The longest freshwater cast recognized by the International Casting Federation is a whopping 574 feet, two inches by Walter Kummerow of West Germany. His record cast came at the 1968 championships in the five- to eight-ounce plug division.

The longest recognized fly cast is 257 feet, two inches by Norway's Sverne Scheen at the same 1968 tournament.